BROTHER SLEEP

BROTHER
SLEEP

ALICE JAMES BOOKS
New Gloucester, ME
alicejamesbooks.org

CONTENTS

BROTHER SLEEP

LITANY WITH BURNING FIELDS

Let's say Death only exists in this line.

Let Sleep be an only child with a single mother: the dark
& elegant moon

dropping poppies into my yawn. In the dream

I burn 600 acres & sprint across the flames
unclothed. I turn out gilded.

I wake up to my brother springing on my bed

before dawn, my grandfather
heating water in the wailing kettle. Again, say Death exists

only in this line: a brother grows tumors in his throat, a grandfather dissolves

into the soil of a churchyard. I admit: I'm in love
with Sleep. Each morning:

I wake up & a shovel caves the peak of my stomach; I wake up

& dust varnishes my brother's side
of the bed; I wake up

& a field is burning outside my window.

1

ENDINGS

This morning I have fog for breakfast.
A whole bank of it. Before sunrise.
Plucked. From the corners of the mountain.

& already I'm thinking about the end.
Of the day. The sunbed unmade.
The lull & the sex of a boy who reminds me.

Of someone I'd rather keep. Unnamed.
The headache after the orgasm. I've been.
Thinking too much about my brother.

Lately. Just how much. Of the day.
He spent asleep before his end.
As if the end. Devoured like voracious fog.

The hours. He had left.
On earth. I want. A different ending.
Or rather a thing that doesn't end.

In heartache. Or headache. The sea.
& the sun. For instance. The quiet. Nestle of clouds.
Falling. Down the pits. Of my body.

AUBADE AT THE CITY OF CHANGE

In this city,
each door I cross
in search of your room

grows darker
than the sky, this silver
dome of morning spread

across the urban smog.
Country dark washes the city
light off the outskirts

& beyond

where you sleep in hiding,
where your face
wrapped in gauze

shines like sequin
in the lingering moon-drizzle.
I reach for you

at the corners of the clubs,
inside motel rooms,

where rent boys tumble
perspired bedsheets,
doubling you, your maleness

discharged,
your hip bones sticking
to my thighs, hard

stubble of your legs
scratching. The night I followed
a strange road, looking

to forget all this, starlight
spooled the gravel ribbon
leading back to the city

behind me, back
to the hospital room
where I last saw you—

tonight, I'll rest
on this road. I'll look back
to the city of change

where one year
two skyscrapers lifted, a park
shed trees

for new thoroughfares,
& an old cinema
erupted to rebuild itself

in its place. I'll stay
on the pavement,
suspended in time

like the broken sign announcing
You are entering _____, (a name

changed two years ago),
& I'll wonder
if the hot breeze

blowing the nape
of my neck
is your unchanged

breath rising like candle
smoke from the city.

INTERROGATION OF THE SODOMITE

In México City, in 1901, police detained 41 gay men at a dance. Many were imprisoned & subjected to labor. Since, in México, the number 41 has been used in jokes & derogatory remarks against gay men.

There are currently six countries where the death penalty is used for people in same-sex relationships: Iran, Saudi Arabia, Sudan, Yemen, Nigeria & Somalia.

1.
Asked to remove my mask, I peeled off my face & let the world see

2.
Inside, a dark made of edges. Asked how I could look myself

3.
In the mirror, I stood before a lake for days, my tongue dry

4.
Stone. I drank all the water. Fish swam inside me

5.
For weeks. Tadpoles shot out my eyes in my sleep. Asked how I could dream

6.
Of men, their waltzing legs, the 41 sharp cheeks blushing in the candle

7.
-lit dark, in México, the 41 abdomens soaking a river with their shame

8.

-less loving, I bit out my tongue, which shot in its silence to bruise & bloody

9.

A loving

10.

Man's forehead

11.

To death in Saudi Arabia today,

12.

Just for loving

13.

The dark

14.

Edges in men.

42

my name was

candlelit

smoke vanished

in a man's silent

inhalation

smoke held

in the pueblo's lungs

I yearn

to keep dancing

in his breath

GLOSSARY FOR WHAT YOU LEFT
UNSAID: PUÑAL

puñal, *adj. desus.*

I hang at the back of the school ground, my fingers
hooked to the chain-link facing the street, tips white

with my body's weight. The oak tree behind me bends
down further each day I visit to smear

my mind on its bark. Armando walks
by the basketball field, spots me. He's surrounded

by boys. He approaches, slow as a hyena & I stab
the lonely tree with another question. Armando spits

on the blacktop, yells *Puñal*—dagger,
                                 faggot, a word
that doubles his voice. That deepens the space

between two countries. This border separating
him from the likes of me. Boys behind him

whistle. They laugh. One of them stabs himself
in the chest with an invisible knife: a gesture that echoes

the word of my erasure. It's afternoon. Early dark.
& before them, the oak tree kneels a little lower.

puñal¹, *m.*

In Ciudad Juárez, always, air tastes bitter with copper,

Coins roll on the mouth, stick to the throats

Of passers-by, hot air rusted & rustling

As they push their way through the city. Downtown

Another body drops on the tarmac—luminous, wet—

His stomach decked with seven slashes

The color of Venus, seven red

Mouths speaking foreign tongues: how the boy walked

Barefoot across La Mariscal, sidewalk broken

Into beer bottles, how the boy walked, how

His whole body waved that curious way & wore

His blue hair down to his shoulders, his hair

An oil slick in the concrete mouth of the alley.

puñal², *m.*

When she learned I'd grow
    To love a man,

My grandmother prayed
    Nine rosaries, the brown beads

Digging the backs of her hands,
    New moles there for me not to end

Like Erykah, in the *El Paso*
    Times, found

By her stepfather in her apartment, her
    Torso bursting

Apertures, 24
    Red orchids rising

Out of her skin. I touched
    My grandmother's back

That night. I knelt
    Beside her, the evening news

In the white background
    & her murmured faith

Effacing each other
    Into noise.

THANATOPHOBIA, OR SLEEP
ADDRESSES HIS BROTHER

No duerme nadie por el mundo.
—*Federico García Lorca*

Night: the world boils. Men
            toss sleepless
                    in their sheets like stars.

            Because I look down
        where a man holds his only son
among the spillage

of buildings & children
            sitting on debris
                    after the bombs

            cast their shadows
        onto stone. There the boy hangs
from his father's arm, his father's hand

folded to the open neck, & the open eyes
            like cold nickels look past me, past
                    the white sheet of linen.

            How terrible
        the fabric that veils
the end. How terrible

the night for him, the sleepless,
Brother. When an American soldier
swallows a grenade which bursts

as it slips down his throat, a Mexican
immigrant, a woman beaten
half to death for stealing

a pomegranate, breaks
the fruit's skin open, red
from her wounds

like the inside of the fruit,
or the inside of the soldier,
& doctors put to sleep

a girl to replace her heart with a new
beating. Soon that artificial
sleep turns the same terrible

fabric. Her mother, quiet
as a desert in the hall,
admires Wojnarowicz's *Untitled*

(*Buffalo*), that great beast at the edge
of the photograph suspended
in air forever.

& the girl's father reaches
her mother's arm to keep her
from plunging off the rooftop

to fall into you,

      Brother. I know nothing

            but impermanent rest.

         How do you do it

      each time you take & take & wrap

your permanence around

sleep? Brother,

     you terrify me.

         You make my heart

         gallop like buffaloes

     in the white desert, their large bodies

advancing their fall.

BANQUET WITH COPPER & RUST

I push two pennies
into the slit of your eyelids

for the ferryman
I've been trying to let go

of you tying a knot to my gullet
to remember you

without shedding—we eat
hot porcelain in shards

pick the splinters off
our teeth with silverware

our mother chokes
on coins & rust

varnishes her vocal cords
I speak to her about my future

children their recurring dream
about the orchard

where each tree sports
a hanging: a dream

knitted from the past
or the near future

what history
unchanged——

I don't want Death
to hang his shadow

over my children
but Brother what stories

can I tell them of you?

INHERITANCE

Mother's hair bundles
in the sunken corner

of the bathtub, is fed
to the drain. Strands

of her youth & her wish
to preserve it. She extinguishes

a candle with water, sizzle
rising to my eardrum, says

her scalp brimmed hair
before my birth, calls me

Ladronzuelo. She brushes
the crown over my temples

white with foam, washes
my slight casket of flesh:

growing organ, harvest
of her body; this vessel

she holds to the surface
in time will shed

a mountain of scabs, stale
rivers of spit & urine,

a dust storm of dead cells—
bone spreading the tented

meat of muscle
& tendon, my skin

unfurling like my mother's
hair into the gutter, organ

of my heart speeding
& slowing—I take

my first step, ride
my first bike, learn

to drive a car, to crash
into strangers

'til they're no longer
strangers, & one

night I'll slip
back into my family

home, my own
hair scarce, to bathe

my mother & lift her
in the blurring

of her mind
to the surface

of hot water,
to foam white her small

crowning, to brush
her shoulders

between the spasms
of her waking,

her eyes
watching me

one more time
before they sink

to the black waters
in her head.

GLOSSARY FOR WHAT YOU
LEFT UNSAID: ART

art¹, *n.*

the boy keeps (to himself) in lunch periods, inside   the unstirred
classroom   maneuvering   wet brushes   over his off-white
canvas   he tints everything different   blues smears a (self-)
portrait with drowned skin   he didn't intend to   look this dead
his eyes stitched   everything wavering under water   water-
color his whole (self)   a month before

art², *n.*

you saw the boy kiss another   boy in the hall.   two weeks later, you

† art, *v.*

saw him creased over the restroom   sink three other boys pressing

his face to the white porcelain   while a fourth   raked his blue

hair with a clipper   you hoisted there   listening

to their laughs the buzz the sink's   screech underneath the boy's

blue fingernails   his hands sunk to the side of his

hips submitting to that loss   of identity   your own

hands fisted   a taste expanding   your palate: licorice

stain on the tongue   you last kissed a silence   swelling like a tumor

in your throat   too large   for both of us   to breathe

CHRONOLOGY WITH LITTLE DEATHS

In the dark screening,
a play of hands, your fingers
blossom in his jeans.

|

Holy water: what
river: our shared bed. Blessing
of your boyhood sleep.

|

The backstreet behind
the theater will do. Broken
bricks. Bruised sky. His face.

|

Seven missed calls. A
voice message you erase. A
man stirring in your bed.

|

Gossip: your neighbor died + last week while having sex + with a woman.

|

Colonies multiply inside you. A temple arches. A rock

|

formation   in your veins   absorbs white

light, your veins   bursting seams.

|

You watch his sperm die
on your hand. He speaks. All you
hear: underwater noise.

|

Gossip: the woman + was not your neighbor's wife.

She wore blue + stockings to the funeral.

|

You play with yourself
again, play yourself into a ditch,

believe love where only lust can bloom, the o
in another man's face, his bareback

|

promise of the ever
after. Lick everything spilled from his quaking

tongue, his word obliterated in your wake—
the sore cheek, the empty bedside.

|

Gossip: the woman might've been your
cousin your + sister your + mother + might've been

|

the moon guiding home
a lost ship, the black sea waves,
the hum of your hips.

2

IMPLODED VILLANELLE

Señor de la Misericordia, Day of the Dead, 2017

[I believe the universe can fit inside an urn | or a casket, or my grandfather's wedding suit embellishing the altar. | & a grain of salt expands, contracts, may burn | the human eye. A scab. Scorn | born out of the ash. When remembrance falters, | the universe is pushed inside an urn | green as arsenic. My smallest brother has outgrown | me: he tumbles into sand, mortar, | & salt: has expanded & contracted: he burns | in the lonely furnace. At home, my bones churn | for the loved & the lovely, still breathing. Mother, | I swear the entire universe fits inside this urn | when blood from the heart clots with yearn, | & constricts the neck, tight as a halter. | My brain, full of salt, expands, contracts, might burst | at its seam: & just like that, I'm dust & scatter. | Tell me, Daughter, who will place my picture in the altar | when the whole universe exists inside an urn | & a grain of salt contracts until it burns?]

OBITUARIES FOR THE UNNAMED

I forget my own grief writing obituaries
      for the unnamed. A mass grave in Ciudad Juárez
            takes fifty more bodies this morning, the gluttonous desert

opening daily its appetite. In a dream, I wander
      into a cave staked with corpses. I produce imprints
            of their faces in my mind. I want

to save them from this brutal coil
      of forgetting. How many of their names their loved ones
            cried? How long ago? I dig

deep into the cave, my brain swollen with faces, & their blood
      pools up my ankles. Listen, the ones whose tongues
            have not been severed want to tell us

their stories: late one night, a woman climbs
      a bus back home from the maquila & ends
            toothless & muzzled in a ditch. She's mothered

a boy without a father, celebrated
      her twentieth birthday in her mother's house
            with cake & cold Coronas. A father leaves

his son & wife to cross the desert
      in the hollowed bottom of a truck. His gut
            hisses in the sun-stunned metal, fighting other bodies

for a breath. Whatever air he wins is stale
      with piss. The truck halts &, quiet, he waits, & waits &—
           the dream ends. I shower. Rinse the salt

off my back. I drink black coffee. Eat cereal. Listen
      to the news. Again, a mass grave opens in Ciudad Juárez,
           & out there, another body flecks the desert's mouth.

SOME NOTES ON LOVE

You are not a shadow. You're not hiding any-
more than the moon in a sleepless city. It's midnight. You're not
breaking or broken. Bent between light

& shade. You are not a shadow bending. You're not hiding
in your room at the family reunion because your hair is the color of the sky &
        they must not love
what the sky looks like. You're not

a bruised eye. A split lip, bleeding. A cracked sidewalk
in a city where a million eyes inhabit the dark. You are not a shadow.
You are not a shadow. You're not

the dark bobbing of a body from a tree in the summer
breeze. Or a dancer punctured by a bullet. No.
You're not a shadow at the edge of a bullet. In the brightest midnight

of the year you are bright smile which should be kissed.
You are sweat & muscle. You are skin & breath. You are blood
which travels the body with its pulse. You are kissed.

GLOSSARY FOR WHAT YOU LEFT UNSAID: GASLIGHT

gaslight, *n. / v.*

look:

an angel: his

plastered dents

a crow's wing:

tall dark stranger

that forged the fissure

his fist

cutting air:

how he changes:

arms extended

to your neck—

the savage

that came

on your face—

against you:

a river of skin:

first he's

for you: he counts

his breath:

darling:

into your life:

he rushes:

a bird plummets:

your dark bruises

GLOSSARY FOR WHAT YOU LEFT UNSAID: BORDER/CITIES

city¹, *n.* densely inhabited arc   in my life, architecture that failed me,
where sirens of police cars dashed   the roads to our houses,
& you built a hiding place   to keep us safe

from the bullets. it rained four consecutive days, flooding the basement—
where amber burned the streets all night, & always,   music
skid past a window or an open door.   at dusk

three corpses littered an avenue. & each thunder rupturing
the sky was a gunshot fired in my mother's tympanum,

          each unanswered phone call, my disappearance.
one night the entire colonia flared with police lights.

          I was inside you
     on the couch,
          in the living room. I felt
               your legs elongating

beneath me, saw your face flash: blue—red—blue—

border, *n.* scaf/   fold supporting our bodies, bent union,
bridge,   where you walked me halfway back to the country

          that deems you illegal,
          our respiration: fog

fermented in whiskey.   you leaned against me,
pissed down the chain-link   where two cites verge,

& bit my lip hard enough to draw blood. we wavered, divided:

         our breaths
         made singular again—

city², *n.* darkly paved   pillar of sun,   where thunder
outside the windowpane is only thunder, & past nine the street remains

quiet & dark. I excavate   another's mouth at the back
of a car, at the high   of a mountain, the lights

of two cities engraving our faces. it's been six years. I turn
a fleeting look to that corner of my country from my fleeting

lover's lips,   past the darkened neighborhoods, the border's
metallic strip   where your house would be: paint charred off

  brick. what distance
     refracts there. what music
  smuggles out the window
    from your room—

WHAT I SAY TO MY MOTHER AFTER HER FATHER DIES IS SOFT

as an organ

liquified beneath a swollen chest—a grenade exploding
in a field. Unbearable. & meaningless. What I mean to say:

there's a mountain at the edge of El Paso bathed in the light
of Ciudad Juárez. I dreamed my grandfather standing there

this morning, wearing only his gold
skin. What I mean to say: let's drive

up the bright road to meet him. But what I say
unloads a carcass on the white bathroom tile. I'm sorry
for my words. I'm sorry, Mother, for only now understanding

how cruel
the sudden leaving, the lack

of a flicker monitoring your father's pulse: your father's pulse
still beeping in the blue. The monitor. Slim morsel of night—

the lack. The beat. The lack. The beat.

I'M AFRAID DOCTORS WILL TELL ME
THE MRI SHOWS:

my inside is coated with holes | stones

clog seven vital organs including my heart | an unidentified creature

dwells the length of my intestine | I'll be dead in nineteen weeks

if not me my father | whom I've never met | if not my father

my mother | who has known me all my life | most of all | I'm afraid

they'll know | three days ago

a married man whose name | he said | was Fernando stapled me inside | a
        rest stop | stall in New Mexico for 196 seconds | kissed me | dumbly
        | dry | & then strutted | away

that a part of him is still lodged in my spleen

GLOSSARY FOR WHAT YOU
LEFT UNSAID: MAD

† mad, *n.*

1.

In my religious high school, a pastor recounted a story he saw on the news about a woman who burned alive her newborn triplets in the oven & woke up, as if from a trance, to find their tiny, charred bodies. The pastor uses this story to prove the existence of the devil.

2.

First time I walked

clasping my lover's hand, my back

itched with stares. I heard

the cracks of revolving necks

shaking their disproval. A sound

of interlocked cogwheels. I crossed

the bridge to El Paso, rotating flesh

still trailing my steps, my hand

    red inside my pocket.

3.

Mother says I was born with a yellow stomach. That I was always a difficult child. Age six: I wouldn't eat anything that wasn't round, afraid of all the edges in my mouth.

4.

In the 17th century, women who spoke to animals or inanimate objects were burned at the stake.

5.

& another cogwheel snaps.

6.

    I carry a sadness like a sibling in my arms,

& though I feel the weight unhinging

    humerus from scapula, I bare it, offer

my bastard brother's scalp the curve

    of my throat. Mornings I condense

back into the world. His concretion

      fastens my extremities to the mattress.

I hear my mother calling & my brother

      shoves harder against me.

7.
Age twelve: I felt earthquakes no one else could feel—the whole house shaking—
the mirror's rattle—the rooftop shedding shingles—

8.
Age fourteen: walls bawled louder than smoke—same noise as an open
window—in a speeding car—people shouting from the avenue—

9.

      Saw you kiss a boy—last night—looked like

you tried—to swallow—his face—swallow

      him whole—his—hole—his—what would your mother say

best—your brother wasn't here—to see

      would've done abuelo—in again—& again

better fix—yourself boy—better fix this—

10.

I've written seven suicide notes: seven yellow pages ending in apology.

11.

& again, there's proof of the devil.

12.

& another cogwheel snaps: my mother shouts—*you are mad* says—*you are mad* says—

13.

14.

I'm sorry.

GLOSSARY FOR WHAT YOU
LEFT UNSAID: LOSS

loss, *n.*

1.

a fireplace heats your head | & the first house you lived stretches | your memory
your past | childhood | at night—

2.

you believed a fat man in a red suit brought you gifts

—despite | you lied to your mother seven times that year | despite—

you bit your tongue until the taste | to keep from spilling:

    a. how a man in your best friend's house asked you
    b. to strip| you climbed| his shirtless| torso in your white under-
    c. wear | the brown fur | in his stomach| the nipple
    d. standing hard—to your touch

† loss, *v.*

1.

how he unloads me:

discharge on the belly—

small whimper & my body

burning water

2.

vessel | &

wreckage |

swollen wood |

ELEGY WITH A DIAL-UP CONNECTION

My grandmother still hears his voice
      in the quiet kitchen. I find her speaking to the dark, sometimes
            tenderly, sometimes cracked in a fit of rage, asking him
                  for one more day in which his voice

booms not from the air but from the face she recognizes
      from old photographs in our living room. I want to believe
            she's gifted. That this disembodied voice
                  is my grandfather calling

out of some diminutive rift in our physical realm
      binding this cluttered room to the unknowable, not
            a glitch in her brain invoking the echo of old
                  memories—(once I turned the light to find her

staring at the unhooked phone, the receiver's hum
      gyrating from its cord down the dining table. Grief
            deepened the creases in her forehead & I wondered
                  if it was the light vanishing my grandfather's shadow,

or the black telephone bringing back the day
      of his dying—[I was not home. I clustered
            alone in the cool of a movie theater, Grandfather's
                yelling hot in my mind. I was not home

when Grandmother heard the blow in the bathroom
      & found him crumpled under the shower, his fingers

white on the loft of his stomach, clasping
his heart from dropping

into sections—{how it had been crumbling since
I'd fought back his disapproval, his voice drilling
holes in my nape, his voice—muy joven pa' saber
lo que es bueno para ti—} I was not home

when she picked up the phone & encountered the brittle
noise of connection, tried, still, to dial an emergency, to rift
the chaos of the digital world, white noise
that devoured my grandfather,

ran to the street, the wind whetted, her eyes
bled by sunlight, stopped the traffic, crying—
I was not home the phone unhooked the pulse
of the line—.]) Today

I sit in the still dark of the kitchen. Incense
disintegrating. Smoke. I inhale. Its seam
hovers the ceramic tiles. & I listen to the dark
for the rasp in my grandfather's voice.

3

SLEEP, BROTHER,

has strange ways of arriving unannounced
since you died. Has been dreamless white,

a series of blanks on a page otherwise
filled with text. Unnecessary

white space   you left.

Brother, I see you
when I wake up. Ghost

of dreams I didn't have or had
forgotten by the time the single fleck of sun

punctured the vein of black sky & blacker
mountaintop. Violet stain on the ceiling

of the city. On the balcony, I remember
my night's waiting for Sleep

to carry you out of the bedroom,
my first lover outside, ready

to slip in. Firm
smell of his

breath on my nostrils. Screech
of the bed & your breath

steaming from the other side

of the room. What dreams
we interrupted with my lover's ending,

that liquid hum. What dreams
when I turned to see you seeing

our limbs under the blankets. What questions
you never asked. Your silence the blank space

I yearned for that night, now
the white slit of air inside my ribs—

BLACK PALACE BLUES

México City's Lecumberri Palace, known as the "black palace," served as a prison from 1900 to 1976. Its "J" section was reserved to imprison gay men, infamous for being used in the detainment of 41 gay men arrested in the dance of 1901.

A.   My skin, for instance, blue for a lack of moon:

B.   Volcanic stone highlighting cells

C.   Blue like Marcelo's lungs spraying the floor

D.   Or the lilacs in my mother's backyard when they hauled me

E.   Out: *por favor, llévenselo por atrás. Que no lo vea la gente.*

F.   Blue like Marcelo's scrotum, which I learned to kiss inside these walls.

G.   Or my spit as a child

H.   Eating ripe moras with my grandfather. I suckle tears from the walls the color of ink—

I.   Blue of our skin lashed for kissing, for not answering back (our last name) when called (by our first).

J.   For no reason other than being. Here. I'm released. I'm blue all over. In seven years, I'll be dead in the alley of a border town & buried under a bed of lilacs, a black word spray-painted onto my gravestone.

GLOSSARY FOR WHAT YOU
LEFT UNSAID: CONCAVE

concave, *n.*

a. a hollow: a cavity: a hiding place: inside the shell of a car: inside the tire: or the seats' gray tapestry: in the lining of a jacket: in the acidy purse of a stomach: the white powder wadding sixty rubber condoms: downed with milk: or pushed into the red velvet lining of an anus: raw flesh: pocketed breasts & buttocks:

refilled: **tb.** I cross full: & empty myself or cold porcelain: cylinder of a gun's of shed bullets:

hollowed out & & recross borders: on cold metal beds: each time the long gullet sings: echoes

> —I'm sorry: but my sister heard a rupture in her stomach this morning: the rubber's softest whisper: undoing: the rest: of her life.

c. because these things are put inside my body: I'm distinctly female in your mind: you keep a gun in the bottom drawer of your room: for safety: here the glass pipe: the pocket mirror: & what I once furrowed down my esophagus: make a line: piston the lightness of smoke: make another line—

MISADVENTURE

To be born
Into the Río
Bravo's current
When the moon
Is high & pink.
To be so small
& round Mother
Mistakes me
For a stone.
To grow up
Without a father.
To blame the fact
Of my faggotry
On being fatherless.
To thank God,
That infinite
Equation, for being
Fatherless.
To know Death
Has two gold teeth
In the front
Of his mouth.
To see him
The night my brother
In his glittering
Fever points
At the corner.
To that grin.

To love a man
Who is a father.
To share his mouth
With his wife.
For an instant.
To lose a friend,
The curving temple
Of his body.
To my touch.
To break
My small
Metacarpal
In a handshake.
I've lost four
Years in my hiding,
Two houses
To the smell
Of gunpowder,
A loved country
For safety.
I know Death
Is as fat, tall,
& white
As the edge
Of this page.

WHAT LIGHT WANTS

In the dim room, the computer
screen beaming, close-up

of a woman's lips, the television
loud with songs retelling

David Bowie's life on film, played
to drown out our flesh,

& moonlight, too, slips in
to take part in our skin,

our softness, this un-
elegant exploration, how we reach

to press our cocks against each other's
in mutual agreement

this would only happen once, even
when light wants: our bodies,

this path we follow: the pores:
the standing hairs: the salt—

GHOSTING

When you left, the arch
      of your body vanished

or swallowed by the desert,
      a gray vulture

clawed into the calico couch
      where you slept. In daylight

the bird clusters inside
      the sponge of a cushion

& sleeps. I sit. I rewatch
      shows I first saw

by your side. I feel the bird
      breathing beneath me.

At night it perches
      on the arm of the sofa

to examine my breath.
      Without you, I often

have dreams of dying
      in the desert, choking

on cacti. Of spines & serpents
  & the vast & yellow sky

that is your absence. Every time,
  the sky spills

into my waking & I
  find the vulture

hovering above.

LOS OLVIDADOS

El CRAEMAC is an asylum for the mentally ill at the outskirts of Ciudad Juárez.

At the desert's edge, a man dangling
large hoop earrings shakes my hand, presents himself

as Juan Gabriel, swears the singer in the TV, in the mariachi outfit, stole

his identity, concealed him in this dry patch of land
where the stench of urine fumes the corners, where he sings

in a high, uneven pitch: *soy honesta con él
& contigo / a él lo quiero & a ti te he olvidado*—

|

Summer exhausts salt
from our pores—riddles us in strange dreams—

at the peak of the season's heat, the violent
are segregated into rooms, stunned

with hypodermics. We scavenge our arms
for sores, the desert air limiting:

we inhale it: the mountain cacti, the spines
clustering our sinuses. We exhale smoke.

|

& again
there's rice
for dinner
& supper.

|

& another winter

outlines the cracks

where our bones

snapped

two decades ago.

|

Daily, for years, a woman clutches the edge
of the iron barrier separating the city. She awaits

her daughter's return. Children
sprint across the sidewalk, outside, rattle

the iron & her fingers.
Her eyes widen. Her lungs

swell for the longest minute: a gush
of wind: the desert rippling inside her.

SINNER

Forgive me, Brother: I sinned. I laughed
     at the joke with the gay priest & the altar boy, missing

the punch line: it's 2018. People still think gay = pedo.
     In my old bedroom I lit incense sticks after fucking Abner

so you wouldn't know. I played straight most of my high school
     years. When I think of Abner, I think

of that 90's Nickelodeon show which played in the background.
     My fist siphoned his white

boxers until the cloth darkened. I tasted salt.
     At Sunday school, an older boy named Andy rocked

his hips furiously, walking. Behind him, boys shadowed
     the sway. Laughed. When he asked me if it was true,

if Abner & I were lovers, I knuckled his face, bent
     cartilage, his snot smeared on my fingers. I liked his face

collapsing under my blow. I liked the other boys
     cheering, behind us, their masculine claps convinced

of the man I was, my red hands unfolded & ready
     to praise God.

PENTECOST, 2006

In the Baptist temple, the cross
   hangs behind the podium,
bodiless. My polluted river
      of thought drowns
the pastor's sermon——: this wood
   lacking flesh: the exposed abs
of Jesus in my Catholic church
   bleeding & fastened
to that symbol. I confess:
      I carry desire in my bones.

A friend crosses & uncrosses
   his legs beside me, bangs
the tip of his shoe
   against my sole, & I turn
to face him, catch first
      the pink scar stitched
above the eyebrow. I'm here
   because he knows
I like the tough fruit in a man's
   throat, & he wants,

like all good Christians want,
      to change this. I'm here
because ten years ago, in his mother's lake
   house, we shared the top
mattress of a bunk bed, beating
   glow-in-the-dark planets

on the wood ceiling. Late
  that morning, I pretended
to sleep. He ran his fingers up my thigh,
 filled me with blood—

Ran. Filled. —I'm here because I want
 a change of tense.
He chews gum. His mandible
  speckles the air. He sings
one last song of worship, shoots
 one last & boring glance
at me, & we scatter
 out the averting parking lot
to the rest of our lives.

GENEALOGY

This is one of seven lies: I grew to love
the absence. Months before I was born, my mother

says, a man came home to dig out the dead
maple tree in the backyard. Says when she was seven

the branch that held her in a swing split, like her knee,
with the fall. I took

my shadow for a sibling
for the longest time. I carried the dead

in my tonsils. One dull midnight
in August, absence

boiled my skin to purple seeds: fevers
high enough to stretch the horizon on my face.

My grandmother pressed the cold
eggshell against my skin. I felt her

prayers shift the air, the candle's burning
in the nightstand, her rosary crackling as she broke

the tainted yolk
into the glass. *Mira,* she said,

& I looked: yellow leaking the red
dot of absence which I bore: my mother's

dead tree: loose soil in the backyard:
my father's face looking back.

BLUE INSOMNIA

Stubborn scrape of vine against glass, my window's bone shutter, & the hymn my grandfather's grandfather

clock intones. Sounds all night—water running—

a bluebird warbles in the trees, & in my mouth: the taste of pennies.

|

Corpses outside my window tap their fingers on the cold glass. Figures blur in rain. & there—there—my grandfather's face trickles from the past.

|

Three black hours I keep tonguing my teeth for copper. There's the shape of a coin under the mattress. I feel it against my vertebrae. I lift the bedding. Find: air. Dry flowers. A black beetle crawling. A spring popping fabric. A rusted razor I used to cut myself in high school.

|

Grandfather slipped quarters between his molars & bit down. Wanted the evenings for himself. Locked the bedroom door

upon which I knocked & knocked until mother found me half asleep on the floor with reddened knuckles.

|

When he lived in a house near a river, Grandfather told me one day we'd build
a boat from the old sycamore & sail

to the Gulf of Mexico. I could sleep. & in my sleep

I traveled the country's vein. I waived past friends & friends of friends, collecting
coins in my pockets. I grew heavy with gold.

|

I woke up sinking.

|

Some nights I want a mouth to kiss, want to fill myself with as much of the
world. Like my grandfather, I want to be torn open with as much of the world.

|

Last night I found a quarter in the gutter & took it

to my mouth. Because I want & want. Because the sky

lacks moon, the rain lacks song, & hunger

hangs a hyacinth at the mouth of my stomach.

4

GLOSSARY FOR WHAT YOU LEFT UNSAID: CITIZEN

citizen, *n.*

a boy like my brother

                crosses a border

to be safe

                cuts a pear in half

remembers his family

                in Honduras

harvesting pears

                his brother

gilded with sweat

                in the brown orchard

his father's skin

                raw with sunburns

his mother asleep

                in the sickbed

in the old house

                he dreams

of his childhood

                the tall gate & the tree

he wakes up

                in a bunk bed

at the shelter

                wet & feverish

this boy who

                like my brother

doesn't want to be

            a flatline——

citizen, *adj.*

D tells me the story of his scar: he's ten & climbing a tree. Picking fruit
from its branches. What he remembers of the fall is the fear

for his weight, the breakability
of wood & bone & gravity's unmerciful

persistence. He doesn't remember the snap, the passing of days, only rising
to his brother's face numb in the corner of the bedroom, & after, not being

able to stand, walk to the restroom, his head
a spigot, spinning ten days straight. Again, D reminds me

of my brother in this story. I imagine his brother as my distant
self, cleansing the stitched wound that plunges his hairline. My brother

wore his scars inside of him. His skin, smooth brightness. I miss him
most after D leaves the shelter: my brain bears a selfish space——

citizen, *v.*

dusk over tornillo——:   the sky   scattering   sparrows

        throbs   & like ash   a blanket   of dark bodies

                                        cascades

                                        on the white tarp   of the tents

LULLABY, AFTER YOU LEFT THE IMMIGRANT SHELTER

I think of you again at the tail end
      of February, after the cage & the tent,

after the fever & the dream about the dream, after 60
      bunk beds in a room & 60 blurred faces

suspended in the dust of the desert,
      after the sleepless

winter & the recurring infection.
      I think of you

standing in this country
      of barbed wire, this country of copper, this

steeped hill you climbed to plant
      on it your dream. I want for you

your own bed in your private
      room in a house where your brother opens

his arms after the dream comes in shades
      of blue from the land of blue

with such longing for the trees
      you climbed

as a child, for your mother's
      lips pressed to your forehead

for your father's rugged palm cupping
      the back of your neck.

ANTI-ELEGY IN THE VOICE OF DEATH

December—another death
            rattle babbles out
    a boy's pharynx, his weight
            numbing his mother's arms,
        hot hunger
     in her breath steaming the street.

She'll awaken
      in an hour, the gap
      between her nose & lip

raw with frostbite. She'll discern
      a new lightness in her son's
          body, the loss
   of something old inside of him,
           & in the thin sword of sun
      she'll know, even before

she attempts to shake his body
      awake: she's no longer
          a mother. She'll begin

yearning for this past state
      of being, plant a black hole
          inside her. People are strange
   like this. She'll consume
          the hollow left in the carcass, nurture it
   like a new offspring, & call it

grief. See, a body is just

        a body—is just

    an orchid blooming

        & wilting & plucked.

SCRAPBOOK FOR MY UNDOING

I'm a red speck
in a blue surface, wanting
to be blue. I promise I tried
my best to keep
my colors in check—

                                         & what a shame

to be seen in this gray light. For the longest time I avoided kissing a mouth
I desired. I desire

                a second chance to open myself. To disrobe & to linger
in my home without bargaining in-

                dignity. How precious, to be nurtured
in a country & a time like this—

From 2008 to 2012, Ciudad Juárez was deemed the most dangerous place on Earth. In its worst year, 3,700 murders were reported, most of them attributed to drug cartels.

But what of the business

of hate? A silence crushes

the city's wind-

pipe. Suddenly, it's hard

to inhale. In the yellow pages

of a newspaper, a victim

shreds their own jugular—

Because they flaunt it

Because they hold hands in front of the children

Because they won't stay silent

Because shameless

Because embrace Because kiss Because family

values Because weaponized public display of affection

I won't admit
a man,
so I'll employ
a metaphor:

His hip bone's
an orchid
embellishing
the unlit suite.

I've never tasted
the ridge
of a flower
before

tonight. Tonight,
the sky is bloody
& attractive.

My brother, in the brown box, died for being—

brother in that white box—

he died for loving—

my brother, in the black box, died—

my father says to say: he died

in a brawl—no—he died

defending his woman—no, my father says to say

he died from immolation—ammunition—a lost bullet—

a strange illness of the blood—in his lungs—inside his throat—

that strange sickness—in his skin—tell them

my father says—   tell them

he didn't die—

un maricón

THE DAY I CAME OUT

      stains flowered

the ceiling

      of my hotel room

where I'd hardly

      slept sun leaked

the inauguration

      of my new decade

& next to me a man

      I didn't know

past the bends

      of his body stirred

I reclined beside myself

      in the shade

to remember

      his face

exalted in my breath

      & how his voice

shook the mounting

      pressures of still

water as he said

      I love you

though he'd never

      seen me before

that night *I love you*

      with his gin

& tonic his winter-

      fresh his navel

piercing his

elongated *O*s
I love you he'd said
      & maybe war ended
with the word
      I turned to his sun-
smoothed torso
      asleep there his
abdomen a road
      map of white space
clavicle shoulder tiny
      bird of a bruise
in the drop
      of his back
& I thought *maybe*
      there's still time
for celebration
      my future a sky
blue terraria
      to display this
ever-burgeoning
      affection not
affliction not
      affectation nor
consequence I
      kissed the man's
forehead & left
      him there
nameless left with no
      number only
the memory of his
      skin & this brilliant
yearning to be
      seen outside

the street pulsed
        shameless so full
of color my body
        broke into a wave
of electricity
        merging seamlessly
with the rest
        of the world

GLOSSARY FOR WHAT YOU
LEFT UNSAID: SILENCIO

silencio[1], *m.*

My brother accidentally swallowed the moon.

        He's yet to speak a word since. He opens his mouth

    & light festers the air with its inconsiderate gleam.

I try to teach him words again.

      Say 'bridge.' Say 'border.' Say 'brother.'

           Light. Light. Light.

silencio[2], *m.*

I resolve to go back to our roots: to our first

              language. In dreams

    I meet an ancestor who wears my mother's eyes, my brother's

        quiet. *Say 'lengua.' Say 'lazo.' Say 'luna.'*

silencio[3], *m.*

My lover, too, swallows the moon,   & I realize

    I'll never escape my family's vices:

    unnecessary light.   At night,

                    I kiss him. The moon

slides like milk down my stomach & I'm sick

with silence. I want everyone to know

       how perfectly our fingers weave to catch dreams.

Say 'I am,' 'I am,' I am.

PRIMER FOR A VIEW OF THE SEA (DIAGNOSIS)

Mesa, AZ, 2002

My brother never saw the sea, except in the grit
of the black & white TV in our hotel room, in the late

hours of his days. Glow
battered his lip, pale emblem

of sores he kept teething
in restless sleep. I don't want to see him there

after I wake alone in a crib
clogged with memory: his palm

jutting out of the pungent dark
where shadows dissected the orange night-

light in our bedroom: the ghosts
I'd formed with my hands. Our mother

swayed in her sheets, beside us, silhouetted
like seamounts. I don't want to see

my brother's head, the streaks of hair
plastered to his forehead, my hand pressing

his curvature to measure
the sickness inside. I don't want to hear

his jaw jittering. His voice thinned
by the swelling. I want only his quiet

awe: the wide take of an empty beach, the ending
of a movie neither of us recognized, that body

of water silvering the air, outlining
seamounts in warm & artificial light.

PRIMER FOR A VIEW OF THE SEA (DESERT)

Ciudad Juárez, CHIH, 2003

I hated, after my brother died, that we'd spend so much time

in the dark, my mother sitting there, a black figure

in the blue night. For weeks, I couldn't sleep. I sat with her, scratching

the leather of the couch, expecting her to scold me not to

get lost in my brother's memory. The living

room stillness brought the halls in the hospital

where I walked by my brother's side, his hand

so light on my shoulder it might've well been air

beneath his robe. I hated, after he'd gone,

that my mother still served three dishes each morning, oatmeal

gone stale by evening, sticky like my brother's throat, the bucket of grime

cupping his sickness. That my mother's body

reflected his: endless

dark around her eyes, her skin protruding

bone, & how the sunlight creased

the lines in her face, her hair wrapped in a turban.

I saw my brother, then, slowly taking into his lungs the hot

summer air. Silently, I watched him breathe.

PRIMER FOR A VIEW OF THE SEA (DREAM)

Ciudad Juárez, CHIH, 2004

To dream I lie in the room that used to be our room,
in the house in which I lost you, that red bungalow
covered in Boston ivy, four weeks before I return
to the sea. This room of wood floors & white
walls dislocates each night to give way to my dreaming.
Tonight, the room becomes a city. Miles of salt
crack under my feet. I look for you here: the city
a black socket on the world's face. Superficial bright
wound. I call your name & the city throws my voice back
across the salt. A wave plummets the horizon. Carries
your voice. A signal lost at sea. Transmission
faint as the song from the broken radio. You say

> *Brother,*
> *I'm here,* & the wave
> grows so near I can taste
> the bitterness of water. Before the wall
> of liquid memory hits, this city
> becomes a room again. Four bare walls & two
> beds, one of them empty. I rise
> to the sound of water trickling
> glass. Has the wave with your return
> swallowed this house whole? The window,
> blurred with rain. The ceiling,
> dripping, wet. I listen

to the rainfall, these footsteps
sticking to the rooftop
of our house.

PRIMER FOR A VIEW OF THE SEA (SLEEP)

El Paso, TX, 2011

At last the tender
    hands of rest
        latch my eyes
           & your bed
           sinks
           into the Rio Grande
        disemboguing
    at the back
of my throat

PRIMER FOR A VIEW OF THE SEA (SHORE)

Matamoros, TAMPS, 2015

some days our dead

glide down

to visit the ocean

they become

so small

in their passing

we mistake them

for the evening breeze

licking our necks

when the shore

darkens empties

& we're left

a single shadow

merging into air

PRIMER FOR A VIEW OF THE SEA (SILT)

Matamoros, TAMPS, 2003

We drive my brother to the Gulf of Mexico, his body
        sand inside a blue basin. I carry him
  & the road slams a pebble against the window
            to interrupt our silence. In a dream,
      we arrive to find sea & sky have traded places. I wake,

    already in Matamoros, my mother resting
behind the steering wheel. Oncoming evening
       softens her face. Here is my brother, still
           in my hand. In the white sand

   of the shore, I give him back
        to my mother. Great Gulf,
          here comes my brother, salt of the earth
     ready to fall into you. My brother:

a body made dust that crawled into my bed in thunder-

       laden nights: a body now scattered. Our way back, silence
      a cave collapsed upon me, & outside
  the river trails this black road home, the arms
         of the ocean in which my brother sleeps.

THIS ROOM WILL STILL EXIST

In the beginning
a field
broke grass

from damp earth
& fertilizer
but crops

would not grow.
The city crept
closer. Before you

& I
were born
our hearts
were ripe

fruit dangling
in a lonely
woman's
backyard.

    |

94 years ago, a stranger slept

with the window open. Fog surged

into his room. Imagine waking

from a dream of sky to sky.

|

Tonight, your face vanished
from my mind's unending
mirror. A blue sadness replaced it.
A sound not your voice,
not your laughter, but the echo
of a gunshot. I strike
my dresser's mirror, break off
a shard the size of your head.

|

There are 86 sadnesses in this room

alone. I've counted each of them: the serpent

standing upright to the height of the ceiling,

the warm bear skulking in the corner, his fur

matted in dust. I've grown a blue

mantis the size of my hands. I've fed it

copper & hyacinth. & often, the black caracara

locked in the closet ululates at night.

|

I'll carry the nightstand, carry
the bed & the desk,
the lamp & the moth circling the lamp

to a new room
in a new country. I'll wear a different tongue.

I'll lacquer the moon. I'll build a bookshelf
from the bark of a dead tree. I'll kiss
a man. I'll kiss a man. I'll kiss

& ask the moon: *when did my brother become myth?*

His face a brown blotch in my dreams.
His skin, particles floating in sunlight.

|

Some dull hour in the future, this alcove

     will be emptied of sound. On a steel table,

in a changing city, my humbled body

     will open for the last time at the hands

of a stranger. I'll love them for this final act

     of surrender. For the kind

stitch & staple. & later, these walls

will hold in them the hum of two lovers,

which is to say two men or two women

burrowing into each other's breath.

NOTES

The first part of the epigraph in "Interrogation of the Sodomite" is a summary of the article "Los 41 y la gran redada" by Carlos Monsiváis, found online in *Letras Libres*. The second part is quoted from the article "US votes against UN resolution condemning gay sex death penalty, joining Iraq & Saudi Arabia" by Tom Embury-Dennis for *The Independent*.

"42" alludes to the alleged 42nd name in the list of men found at the dance of the 41, Ignacio de la Torre y Mier, son-in-law of president Porfirio Díaz.

"Glossary for What You Left Unsaid" poems are inspired by the definitions of their respective words from the *Oxford English Dictionary* & the *Real Academia Española*.

The epigraph in "Thanatophobia, or Sleep Addresses His Brother, Death" is from Federico García Lorca's poem "Ciudad sin sueño."

"Glossary for What You Left Unsaid: Puñal" references Erykah Tijerina, a trans woman stabbed to death by Fort Bliss soldier Anthony Michael Bowden on August 2016 in El Paso, TX. Details of the crime come from articles written by Aaron Martinez for *El Paso Times*.

"Some Notes on Love" is written after Diannely Antigua's poem of the same name.

"Elegy with a Dial-Up Connection" is for my grandfather, Martín Amparán.

"Glossary for What You Left Unsaid: Border / Cities" is for Luis Alonso.

The epigraph in "Black Palace Blues" summarizes information from the article

"El palacio negro que inventó a los 'jotos,'" written by Magalli Delgadillo for *El Universal*.

Lyrics quoted in "Los Olvidados" come from the song "Así Fue" by Juan Gabriel.

"Scrapbook for my Undoing" borrows a slightly modified quote from the article "Once the World's Most Dangerous City, Juárez Returns to Life," written by Sam Quinones for *National Geographic*. The italicized section is composed of online comments (translated from the Spanish & slightly modified to fit the anaphora) from users opposing LGBTQIA+ rights in favor of "traditional family values."

"Primer for a View of the Sea (Desert)" begins & ends with slightly modified lines by Sharon Olds.

"This Room Will Still Exist" takes its title from a line in Charlie Kaufman's film *Synecdoche, New York* (2008).

ACKNOWLEDGMENTS

Thank you to the editors of the following publications where these poems, some of them in earlier versions, first appeared:

The Academy of American Poets' *Poem-a-Day:* "Aubade at the City of Change"

The Adroit Journal: "Sinner" & "Genealogy"

Black Warrior Review: "Glossary for What You Left Unsaid: Border / Cities"

BOAAT: "Glossary for What You Left Unsaid: Gaslight"

Cherry Tree: "Black Palace Blues" & "Litany with Burning Fields"

Cream City Review: "Imploded Villanelle"

Foglifter: "Glossary for What You Left Unsaid: Mad" & "Scrapbook for My Undoing"

Foundry: "This Room Will Still Exist"

Fugue: "Thanatophobia, or Sleep Addresses His Brother"

Gulf Coast: "Glossary for What You Left Unsaid: Art"

Hobart: "What Light Wants"

The Journal: "Chronology with Little Deaths"

Kenyon Review Online: "Interrogation of the Sodomite"

Meridian: "Glossary for What You Left Unsaid: Loss"

Ninth Letter: "Misadventure"

Parentheses: "Banquet with Copper & Rust"

The Pinch: "Glossary for What You Left Unsaid: Silencio" & "I'm afraid doctors will tell me the MRI shows:"

Ploughshares: "Glossary for What You Left Unsaid: Puñal"

Poet Lore: "Anti-Elegy in the Voice of Death" & "Pentecost, 2006"

Poetry Northwest: "Glossary for What You Left Unsaid: Concave"

Puerto del Sol: "Blue Insomnia" & "Ghosting"

Quarterly West: "Obituaries for the Unnamed"

The Rumpus: "The Day I Came Out"

Salt Hill: "Primer for a View of the Sea (Diagnosis)"

Sonora Review: "Los Olvidados"

The Southampton Review: "Glossary for What You Left Unsaid: Citizen"

Southeast Review: "Endings"

Washington Square Review: "Sleep, Brother,"

"Thanatophobia, or Sleep Addresses His Brother" was selected by guest editor Brian Teare to appear in *Best New Poets 2020*.

"Glossary for What You Left Unsaid: Border/Cities," "Inheritance," "Litany with Burning Fields," "Los Olvidados," & "Misadventure" were part of Xochitl Rodriguez's art exhibition, *Grown Without Water*, at Mid-America Arts Alliance.

Enormous bounties of gratitude—

to Sasha Pimentel, for her patience, devotion, & outstanding mentorship throughout the creation of this book.

to Carey Salerno, Alyssa Neptune, Julia Bouwsma, Andrés Cerpa, & everyone at Alice James Books for making this book possible.

to my friends, colleges, & mentors who have inspired, supported, & held me during the writing of this book—Rosa Alcalá, Daniela Armijo, Andrea Blancas Beltran, Daniel Chacón, Bill Clark, John Compton, Dennis Cooper, Andrea Cote Botero, Gabriel Dozal, Maria Esquinca, Ysella Fulton-Slavin, Sergio Godoy, Rigoberto González, Saúl Hernández, Cassie Holguin-Pettinato, H.M. Huízar, Lupe Mendez, Oscar Moreno, Alessandra Narváez Varela, Irma Nikicicz, jj peña, José de Piérola, Daniela Ruelas, Donna Snyder, & Lex Williford.

to the organizations & institutions that have provided time, space, & resources to write this book—the Bilingual MFA in Creative Writing program at the

University of Texas at El Paso, CantoMundo, & the National Endowment for the Arts.

& to my family, blood & otherwise, with love—to my mother, Ofelia; my grandmother, Coco; my aunt, Rebeca—& to Luis Alonso Araiza, Cleo Arévalo, Guido Armendariz, Francisco Barraza, Norma Canales, Irvinn Ceja, Raul Hardin, Guillotina Hernández, Lidia Macias, Jorge Manzanilla, Mario Martz, Cinthia Moreno, Esther Olivares, & Berenice Zepeda.

RECENT TITLES FROM ALICE JAMES BOOKS

Alice James Books is committed to publishing books that matter. The press was founded in 1973 in Boston, Massachusetts as a cooperative, wherein authors performed the day-to-day undertakings of the press. This element remains present today, as authors who publish with the press are invited to collaborate closely in the publication process of their work. AJB remains committed to its founders' original feminist mission, while expanding upon the scope to include all voices and poets who might otherwise go unheard. In keeping with its efforts to build equity and increase inclusivity in publishing and the literary arts, AJB seeks out poets whose writing possesses the range, depth, and ability to cultivate empathy in our world and to dynamically push against silence. The press was named for Alice James, sister to William and Henry, whose extraordinary gift for writing went unrecognized during her lifetime.

Designed by Alban Fischer

Printed by McNaughton & Gunn

ALDO
AMPARÁN

10 9 8 7 6 5 4 3 2 1

Alice James Books are published by Alice James Poetry Cooperative, Inc.

Alice James Books
Auburn Hall, Suite 206
60 Pineland Drive
New Gloucester, ME 04260
www.alicejamesbooks.org

Library of Congress Cataloging-in-Publication Data

Names: Amparán, Aldo, author.
Title: Brother sleep / Aldo Amparán.
Description: New Gloucester, ME : Alice James Books, 2022
Identifiers: LCCN 2022012121 (print) | LCCN 2022012122 (ebook)
   ISBN 9781948579278 (trade paperback) | ISBN 9781948579360 (epub)
Subjects: LCGFT: Poetry.
Classification: LCC PS3601.M725 B76 2022 (print) | LCC PS3601.M725 (ebook)
   DDC 811/.6—dc23/eng/20220328
LC record available at https://lccn.loc.gov/2022012121
LC ebook record available at https://lccn.loc.gov/2022012122

Alice James Books gratefully acknowledges support from individual donors,
private foundations, the National Endowment for the Arts, and the Amazon
Literary Partnership. Funded in part by a grant from the Maine Arts Commission,
an independent state agency supported by the National Endowment for the Arts.

Cover art: "Variation 7" from *Intimacy Hierarchies (The Annunciation)*
by Luis González Palma, inkjet print on watercolor paper